Australian Animals
Koalas

ABDO Publishing Company

by Julie Murray

Big Buddy BOOKS
Australian Animals

VISIT US AT
www.abdopublishing.com

Published by ABDO Publishing Company, 8000 West 78th Street, Edina, Minnesota 55439.

Copyright © 2012 by Abdo Consulting Group, Inc. International copyrights reserved in all countries. No part of this book may be reproduced in any form without written permission from the publisher. Big Buddy Books™ is a trademark and logo of ABDO Publishing Company.

Printed in the United States of America, North Mankato, Minnesota.
052011
092011

PRINTED ON RECYCLED PAPER

Coordinating Series Editor: Rochelle Baltzer
Editor: Marcia Zappa
Contributing Editors: Megan M. Gunderson, BreAnn Rumsch, Sarah Tieck
Graphic Design: Maria Hosley
Cover Photograph: *Corbis*.
Interior Photographs/Illustrations: *Getty Images*: AFP (p. 9); *Glow Images*: Max Earey (p. 9); *iStockphoto*: ©iStockphoto.com/benjamint444 (p. 27), ©iStockphoto.com/CraigRJD (p. 17), ©iStockphoto.com/Matejay (p. 4), ©iStockphoto.com/TimothyBall (p. 4); *Photolibrary*: Aflo Foto Agency (p. 13), Bios (pp. 11, 15), Oxford Scientific (OSF) (pp. 15, 19, 27), Peter Arnold Images (pp. 8, 17, 25, 26), Wildlife (p. 7); *Shutterstock*: Paul Coartney (p. 5), Max Earey (p. 9), Eric Isselée (p. 12), kaarsten (p. 29), Robyn Mackenzie (p. 22), markrhiggins (pp. 21, 23), Photoinjection (p. 29), Tijmen (p. 11).

Library of Congress Cataloging-in-Publication Data

Murray, Julie, 1969-
  Koalas / Julie Murray.
      p. cm. -- (Australian animals)
  ISBN 978-1-61783-012-9
  1. Koala--Juvenile literature. I. Title.
  QL737.M384M87 2011
  599.2'5--dc22
                                          2011002305

Contents

Amazing Australian Animals 4
Koala Territory 6
Welcome to the Continent Down Under! 8
Take a Closer Look 10
Life in Trees 14
Good Climbers 16
Lonely Life 18
Mealtime 20
Baby Koalas 24
Survivors 28
Crikey! I'll bet you never knew... 30
Important Words 31
Web Sites 31
Index 32

Amazing Australian Animals

Long ago, nearly all land on Earth was one big mass. About 200 million years ago, the land began to break into **continents**. One of these is an island called Australia.

Koalas live in trees.

Living on an island allowed Australian animals to **develop** separately from other animals. So today, many are unlike animals found anywhere else in the world! One of these animals is the koala.

Koala Territory

There are two types of koalas. These are northern koalas and southern koalas. Both live in the eucalyptus (yoo-kuh-LIHP-tuhs) forests of eastern Australia.

Uncovered!
Eucalyptus trees are common in Australia. There, they are known as eucalypts, gum trees, or stringybark trees.

Koala Territory

Large eucalyptus trees provide a safe home and food for koalas.

Welcome to the Continent Down Under!

If you took a trip to where koalas live, you might find...

...mountains.

The Great Dividing Range is Australia's largest mountain range. It runs along the continent's east coast. Koalas live in its forests.

...the Australia Zoo.

This famous zoo in Beerwah, Queensland, is a popular place to visit. It is home to Australian animals, such as koalas. Animals from around the world also live there.

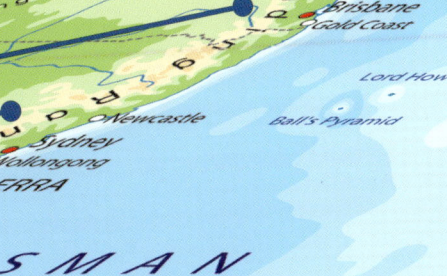

...Aborigines.

The earliest-known people to live in Australia were the Aborigines (a-buh-RIHJ-nees). The name *koala* comes from an Aboriginal word meaning "no drink."

Take a Closer Look

Koalas have broad faces with large, leathery noses and round, furry ears. They have long **digits** and sharp claws. Koalas do not have tails.

Koalas have thick fur. This keeps them from getting too hot or too cold. Gray or brown fur covers a koala's back. White fur is on its belly, under its arms, and inside its ears.

Uncovered!
Southern koalas have thicker fur than northern koalas. Scientists believe this keeps them warm in the south, where the weather is cooler.

A koala's fur is soft and woolly like a sheep's wool.

A koala's fur helps it stay dry in the rain.

Koalas grow to be two to three feet (0.6 to 0.9 m) long. Northern koalas weigh 10 to 20 pounds (5 to 9 kg). Southern koalas are slightly heavier. They weigh 15 to 30 pounds (7 to 14 kg).

Koalas have small eyes compared to their other features. So, they can't see very well. But, they have strong senses of smell, hearing, and touch.

A koala has a large head for its body size.

Uncovered!
Adult male koalas are usually bigger than adult females.

Life in Trees

Koalas spend almost their whole lives in trees. They only come down to move to different trees.

Koalas are very slow movers. They are mostly active at night. During the day, they sleep tucked into the forks of trees. Koalas may sleep up to 20 hours a day!

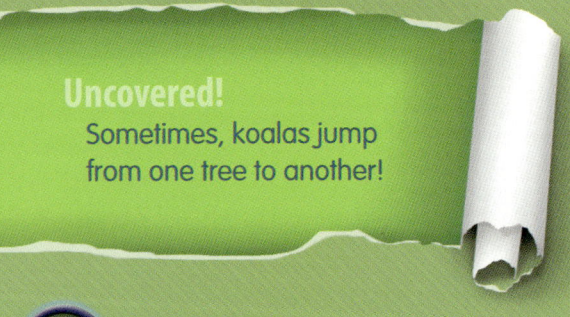

Uncovered!
Sometimes, koalas jump from one tree to another!

In trees, koalas (*left*) are hidden from predators. These include wild dogs called dingoes (*below*).

Good Climbers

Koalas are built for climbing. They have strong front legs and paws. Koalas have thumb-like **digits**, which help them hold branches. And, the skin on the bottom of their feet is **rough**. This keeps them from slipping.

Uncovered!
Koalas can climb to the tops of trees that are 150 feet (46 m) tall!

Koalas use their long, curved claws to hold onto branches.

Lonely Life

Koalas generally live alone. Each one has its own home trees. Koalas like a lot of space. Usually, they have about 100 home trees each!

Koalas sometimes visit each other's home trees. They do this to **mate**. And, koala mothers share their home trees with their babies.

Uncovered!
Even though koalas live alone, they have many ways to share their feelings. They make low, grunting yells when angry. When scared, koalas may scream like human babies. And, mother koalas may make quiet clicking or humming sounds to their babies.

A koala uses its scent to mark its home trees. This lets other koalas know the trees are taken.

Mealtime

Koalas eat the leaves of the eucalyptus trees they live in. Australia has more than 500 types of eucalyptus trees. But, koalas only eat from about 35 of them.

Koalas rarely drink water. Eucalyptus leaves have a lot of water in them. So, koalas get the water they need from their food.

Koalas eat a lot for their size. An adult koala eats one to three pounds (0.5 to 1.4 kg) of eucalyptus leaves a day!

Eucalyptus leaves are firm and leathery. They would be hard for some animals to chew. But, koalas have special cheek teeth. They use them to chop up the leaves before swallowing.

Eucalyptus leaves are poisonous to most animals. But, koalas can **digest** them safely. Special **bacteria** in their stomachs breaks down the plant's poison.

Eucalyptus Leaf

It takes a lot of time and effort for koalas to digest eucalyptus leaves. That's one of the reasons koalas are so slow and sleepy!

Baby Koalas

Koalas are part of a group of **mammals** called marsupials (mahr-SOO-pee-uhls). Marsupials have tiny babies called joeys. Joeys are born before they are done **developing**. A newborn joey lives inside a special pouch on its mother's belly. There, it continues growing.

Female koalas have pouches that open toward their back legs.

A newborn koala joey is about the size of a jelly bean. It weighs less than 0.1 ounces (3 g).

Uncovered!
Scientists believe ancient koalas lived in homes they dug into the ground. Having pouches that opened toward the back legs helped keep dirt out while digging.

Female koalas usually give birth to one joey at a time. A newborn koala joey crawls inside its mother's pouch. There, it drinks its mother's milk and grows.

After five to seven months, a joey first comes out of its mother's pouch. It clings to its mother's belly or rides on her back. Soon, it begins to eat eucalyptus leaves.

A koala joey stays with its mother for one to three years. During this time, it returns to her pouch often to eat, sleep, or hide.

Survivors

Koalas face many dangers. Dingoes, eagles, and owls hunt them for food. Years ago, people hunted koalas for their fur. Over time, much of their **habitat** has been cut down for buildings and farmland.

Still, koalas **survive**. Today, it is against the law to kill them. And, many people work to save their habitat. Koalas help make Australia an amazing place!

Uncovered!
Scientists believe there are about 40,000 to 80,000 koalas living in the wild.

In the wild, koalas live 10 to 15 years.

Cars are another danger koalas face. Staying up in trees keeps them safe.

Crikey!
I'll bet you never knew...

...that koalas are not bears. Koalas look like soft, cuddly teddy bears. And, they are sometimes called koala bears. But, they are not even related to bears!

...that koalas and humans are the only animals that have individual fingerprints. Like with people, you can tell one koala apart from another by looking at their fingerprints.

...that koalas eat dirt. This helps them **digest** their food.

Important Words

bacteria (bak-TIHR-ee-uh) tiny one-celled organisms that can only be seen through a microscope. Some are germs.

continent one of Earth's seven main land areas.

develop to go through steps of natural growth.

digest (deye-JEHST) to break down food into parts small enough for the body to use.

digit (DIH-juht) a finger or a toe.

habitat a place where a living thing is naturally found.

mammal a member of a group of living beings. Mammals have hair or fur and make milk to feed their babies.

mate to join as a couple in order to reproduce, or have babies.

rough (RUHF) not smooth.

survive to continue to live or exist.

Web Sites

To learn more about koalas, visit ABDO Publishing Company online. Web sites about koalas are featured on our Book Links page. These links are routinely monitored and updated to provide the most current information available.

www.abdopublishing.com

Index

Aborigines **9**

Australia **4, 5, 6, 8, 9, 20, 28**

Australia Zoo **9**

body **10, 12, 13, 16, 17, 22, 24, 25, 26, 27**

climbing **16**

communication **19**

dangers **15, 28, 29**

dingoes **15, 28**

eagles **28**

eating habits **7, 20, 21, 22, 23, 26, 27, 30**

eucalyptus trees **6, 7, 20, 21, 22, 23, 26**

fur **10, 11, 28**

Great Dividing Range **8**

habitat **5, 6, 8, 28**

homes **5, 7, 14, 18, 19, 20, 25**

joeys **18, 19, 24, 25, 26, 27**

mammals **24**

marsupials **24**

mating **18**

northern koalas **6, 10, 12**

owls **28**

size **12, 13, 21, 25**

southern koalas **6, 10, 12**